SLIMY SCIENCE

and

AWESOME EXPERIMENTS

Amazing tests and tricks!

✩ Susan Martineau

Illustrated by Martin Ursell

b small publishing
www.bsmall.co.uk

Contents

Before You Begin

Most of the experiments give you pretty immediate and stunning results. Some of them take longer and need more patience — but they are worth it!

You don't need any special equipment to do the experiments. They use things you will probably have about the house already — like old bottles, vinegar, tinfoil, scissors, paper, and so on.

Read through the whole experiment before you begin. If it doesn't work the first time, try again! You could keep notes or even draw up your results like a real professional.

Remember never to play with heat or chemicals, and don't forget to tidy up afterwards!

Always ask a grown-up for permission before you start. Sometimes you will need a bit of adult help.

Sense-sational Science

Our senses of smell, sight, touch and taste all play a vital part in telling us what things are. Is it edible? Is it fresh or stale? Is it bitter or sweet? See what happens when you can't use all of your senses to identify things.

Squidge 'n Sniff

Get your friends squelching their fingers in gunge! You can choose your own gunky ideas too but remember to make sure no one tastes the stuff. Just squidge and sniff!

What you will need:

- 5 small bowls or saucers
- 5 different squidgy substances, e.g. honey, mustard, shampoo, ketchup, toothpaste
- scarf
- tissues

This makes a great party game – especially at Halloween.

In each bowl or saucer dollop a different substance. Make sure your friends are not looking.

Lightly blindfold a brave friend with the scarf. Hold their finger and stick it into one of the substances.

Ask your friend to sniff the stuff on their finger and tell you what they think it is. Wipe the finger and try the next bit of gunge.

Weird or What?

One of the pongiest flowers ever is also the largest in the world. The rafflesia flower measures up to 1 metre across and is found in Malaysia and Indonesia. It might look lovely but it smells like rotting meat!

Tricky Tastebuds

This is a tricky test for your tastebuds. Try it out on your family and friends. You could think of other foods to sample too.

What you will need:
- potato
- apple
- cucumber
- peeler and knife
- plate
- kitchen towel
- scarf

FACT FILE ▷▶

Your tastebuds are amazing! Touch the tip of your tongue with a clean, wooden lolly stick and the wood will taste sweet. At the sides of your tongue it will taste sour. Right at the back (careful!) it will taste bitter.

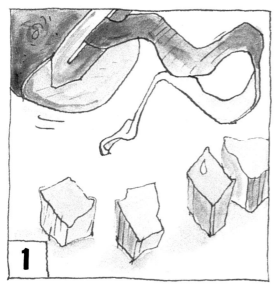

1

Peel the fruit and veg. Cut a few chunks of each. Make them about the same size.

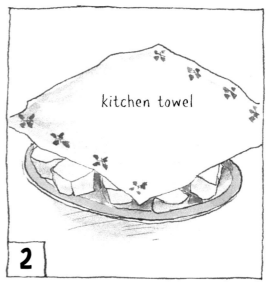

kitchen towel

2

Put the chunks on a plate and cover them up. Do not let anyone see which is which.

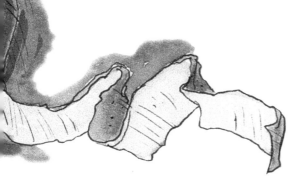

Weird or What?

When it is slurping up bugs, a toad can flick its tongue out and back again in one tenth of a second.

3

Lightly blindfold a friend and ask them to hold their nose. Feed them a piece of each food and see if they can tell you what it is.

Bouncing Light

Mirrors are great for magic effects. By holding them in different positions next to pictures or photos you can make things look very strange.

What you will need:
- glue
- passport photo of yourself (from a photo booth)
- small rectangular make-up mirror

1 Glue your photo on top of the face in the box opposite. Make sure the top of your head lines up with the horizontal line, and your nose is over the vertical one.

2 Stand one edge of the mirror on the vertical dotted line. Gradually slide it to the right — and you've conjured up a twin!

3 Now place the mirror on the horizontal line and — wow! — you're doing acrobatics.

Weird or What?

Modern-day mirrors are made of a sheet of glass with a very thin coat of silver on the back. Before they were invented, people used polished metal to check how bad their spots were! For some weird reflections, look at yourself in each side of a shiny spoon.

Glue your photo on top of this face, in the same position.

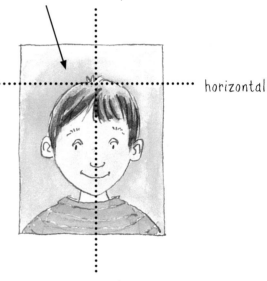

horizontal

vertical

FACT FILE ▷▷

In this experiment you see the photo in two different ways. When you look at the picture itself, light bounces directly off the photo into your eyes. But the image you see in the mirror is light bouncing off the photo, on to the shiny surface of the glass, and then into your eyes.

If you have two small mirrors, stand them on their edges facing each other, on each side of the photo. Count how many of you you can see.

Mighty Magnifier

Make a simple magnifying glass. All you need is some card and clingfilm.

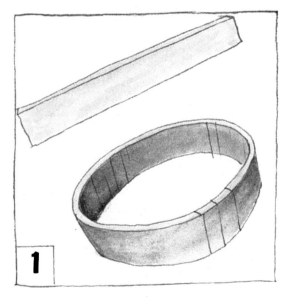

What you will need:

- card or empty sticky tape roll (any size)
- scissors
- clingfilm
- sticky tape
- a dead insect (optional)

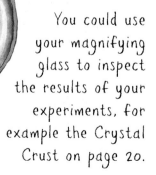

You could use your magnifying glass to inspect the results of your experiments, for example the Crystal Crust on page 20.

1

If using card, cut a strip about 15 cm long. Tape the ends together to make a circle.

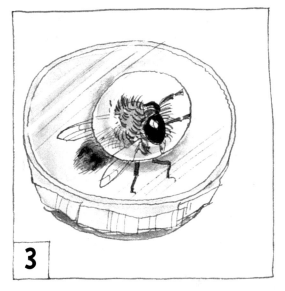

2 Cut a piece of clingfilm big enough to cover and overlap the edges of the circle or empty roll. Keep it taut and tape round sides.

3 Place the magnifier over the insect or the drawings below, and gently plop a few drops of water on to the clingfilm surface. Look through the water at the superbugs!

FACT FILE ▷▶
The glass lens of a magnifying glass is curved and changes the angle of the rays of light. This makes things look larger and more detailed. Here the water on the clingfilm works like a lens.

Eggsperiments

You can do some great experiments using eggs. The first one is not for the faint-hearted!

Floating Eyeball

What you will need:

- 1 uncooked fresh egg
- waterproof felt-tip pens
- large glass jam jar
- tablespoon
- lots of salt

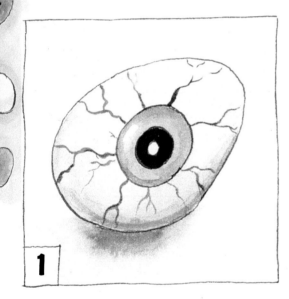

1

Draw an eyeball on the egg using the felt-tips. Let the ink dry.

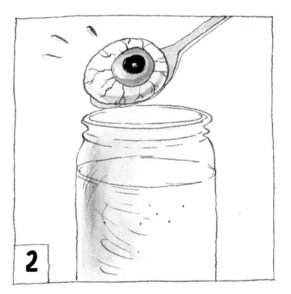

2

Fill the jam jar with very warm water. Gently lower the egg into the jar using the spoon.

3

Gradually stir one tablespoon of salt after another into the water and watch that eyeball begin to lift off the bottom. Ugh!

The Fresh Egg Test

Place an uncooked egg in a glass bowl of water. If it lies down horizontally then it is fresh. If one end starts to rise to the surface this means the egg has more air inside it and is not so fresh. An egg that stands up is stale!

FACT FILE ▷▶

Just as the salt in the sea holds you up when you are swimming, the salty water supports the weight of the egg. The saltier the water the better it will float.

DEAD SEA

The Incredible Rubber Egg

How do you take the shell off
a hard-boiled egg without cracking it?
It's very simple and here's how.

What you will need:
- 1 hard-boiled egg, with shell on
- glass of vinegar

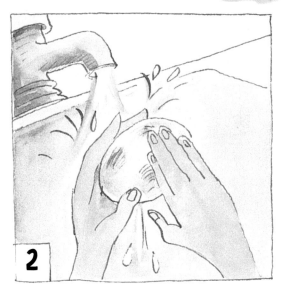

Put the egg into the vinegar.
Leave it undisturbed for 3 days.
You will see some wonderful scum!

Take the egg out of the vinegar
and rinse it off. The shell will rub
off as you wash it.

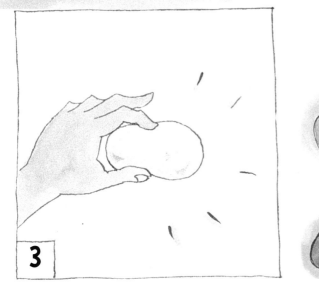

3

Give the egg a poke with your finger.
Squeeze it gently. What does it feel
like? It may even bounce!

FACT FILE ▷▶

The acid vinegar
'eats up' the calcium
carbonate shell, just
leaving the inner
membrane, or skin,
of the egg behind.
This makes it feel
very rubbery.

Salty Stuff

The Magic Ice Cube

Amaze your friends and family with this cool trick.

What you will need:

- 1 ice cube
- glass of cold water
- 15 cm length of sewing thread
- salt
- teaspoon

Gently pop the ice cube into the glass of water. Carefully place one end of the thread across the top of the floating cube.

Where the thread touches the ice, sprinkle salt over it with the spoon.

3

Wait for about 30 seconds and carefully lift the string. The cube will come too.

FACT FILE ▷▶

Because salt lowers the freezing point of water, it melts the ice a little. The thread sinks into a little pool of water which refreezes, trapping the thread.

Weird or What?

If you piled up all the salt in the world's oceans and seas, it would cover the whole of Europe with a salt mountain 5 km deep.

Weird or What?

Believe it or not, one litre of blood has the same amount of salt in it as one litre of sea water!

Crystal Crust

Salt is made of tiny grains, or crystals. You can make your own colony of salt crystals. Don't forget to ask a grown-up to help with the hot water stage of this experiment.

What you will need:
- 1 thick plastic beaker
- boiling water
- salt
- tablespoon
- piece of paper or kitchen towel

Take care! Hot!

1

Ask a grown-up to help you fill the beaker with boiling water. Stir in 2-3 tablespoons salt. Keep adding salt until no more will dissolve.

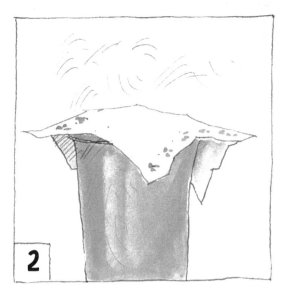

2

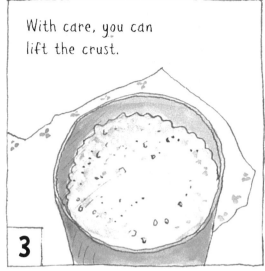

With care, you can lift the crust.

3

Cover the beaker with the paper or kitchen towel, and leave the water to cool. Wait for about 30 minutes.

Lift the paper and you will see a lovely, solid crust of salt crystals on top of the water.

FACT FILE ▷▶

Salt crystals will dissolve more easily in warm water than in cold. As the water cools down, some of the salt that dissolved when the water was warm turns back into crystals again.

You can use the magnifier on page 12 to look at the salt crystals more closely.

Whizz, Bang, Burp

Ghastly Gassy Creatures

Watch these monsters expand before your eyes! You can make a whole family of them if you like. Make your designs as big as possible on the unblown-up balloons. To make your own stickers, colour in and cut out plain sticky labels.

What you will need:

- balloons
- bought or home-made gruesome stickers (e.g. eyeballs, fangs)
- small funnel
- teaspoon
- bicarbonate of soda
- vinegar
- small, empty, clean bottles

Vinegar stings your eyes, so take care. Wash any spillages with plenty of water.

You could try some of these ghastly ideas.

FACT FILE ▷▷

When the bicarbonate falls into the vinegar it causes a chemical reaction which produces carbon dioxide gas. This then blows up the balloon for you.

22

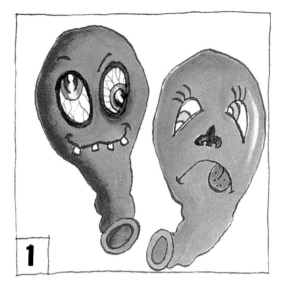

1

Position your stickers firmly on each balloon. Make horrible faces or creatures.

Tap the funnel to help it go down.

2

Using the funnel, spoon 3 heaped teaspoons of bicarbonate into each balloon.

3

Fill each bottle, a third full, with vinegar and fit the neck of a balloon over each one. Don't let any bicarbonate fall in yet.

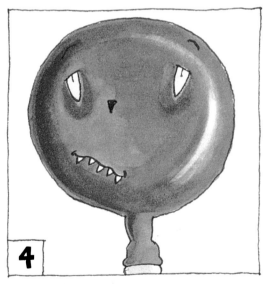

4

Now hold each balloon up and let all the bicarbonate fall into the vinegar.

23

Balloon Belcher

A simple and safe chemical reaction means you can create some very satisfying sound effects. The vinegary smell makes it even more realistic!

What you will need:
- 1 gassy creature from previous page

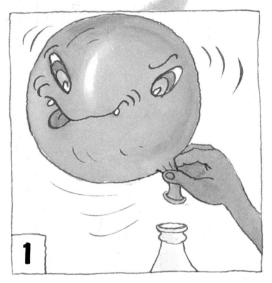

1 Carefully ease the balloon, full of gas, off the bottle. Hold the end tightly closed.

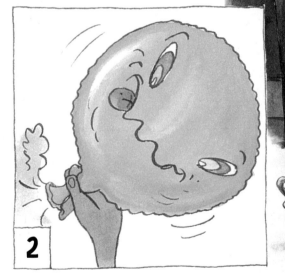

2 Slowly let some gas out to make the balloon burp. Practice will make perfect!

Weird or What?

Bacteria in your intestines can produce as much as 1 litre of gas each day!

Slimy World

Create a slithery worm paradise. To find your slimy friends look in freshly dug soil, under large stones and logs, or anywhere damp and shady. See if you can spot worm casts — swirls of earth made as soil passes through a worm's body — deposited on the surface.

What you will need:
- shoe box with lid
- sticky tape
- pencil
- large empty plastic bottle
- scissors
- 3-4 large beakers of soil
- 1-2 large beakers of sand
- leaves and grass
- 3-4 fat earthworms

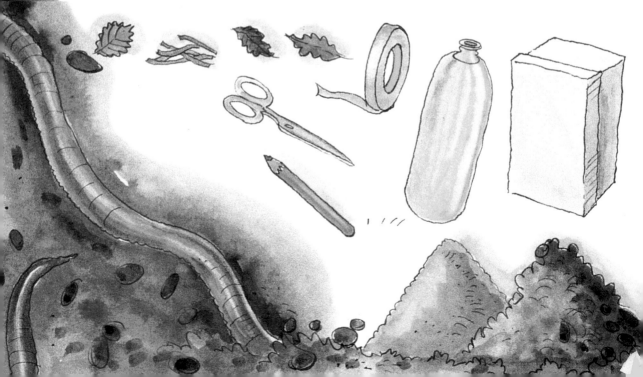

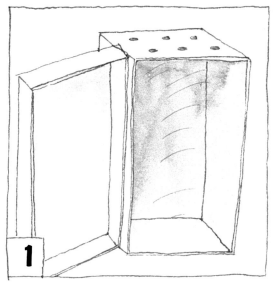

1

Tape the lid to the box to make a 'door'. Push the pencil into the top of the box to make air holes.

2

Ask an adult to help with cutting.

Don't make it too damp.

Cut the top off the bottle and fill it with alternating layers of soil and sand. Sprinkle with water.

Handle your worms gently.

3

Place some leaves and grass on top. Gently place your worms on them.

FACT FILE ▷▶

Worms are the gardener's friend. They pull vegetation down into the soil which makes it rich in nutrients for plants. Their tunnels let air and water into the earth, too.

4

Put the bottle in the box and close the 'door'. Leave in a shed or cool, dark place for 4-5 days.

5

Open the 'door' and you will see your worms have made tunnels through the soil and sand layers and pulled some food down with them.

WORM HEALTH WARNING
Please set your worms
free after a few days!

Weird Worm Fact

Some of the largest earthworms on earth are found in Australia. The Giant Gippsland Earthworm can grow up to 2 metres in length. Just think how much soil a worm that size can shift!

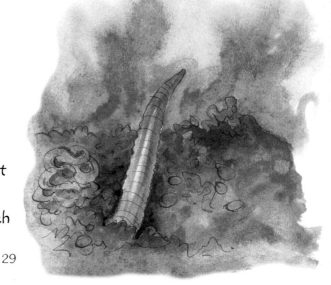

Volcanic Eruption

Make your own volcanic special effects using the simplest of ingredients. It's best to wear old clothes while doing this experiment, and to do it outside.

What you will need:

- old newspapers
- damp sand
- bicarbonate of soda
- small bottle
- funnel
- vinegar
- tomato ketchup
- tablespoon
- small jug

Weird or What?

The greatest volcanic eruption ever recorded was on the island of Krakatoa in Indonesia in 1883. The sound of it was heard 5,000 km away in Australia and it made a gigantic tidal wave that killed more than 36,000 people. The wave was even noticed as far away as the English Channel!

The sand should come up to the top of the bottle.

1

Half fill the bottle with the bicarbonate. Then stand it on the newspapers and mound up the sand around it to form a small volcano.

2

Put about half the small bottle's worth of vinegar in the jug and mix in about 2 tablespoons of ketchup.

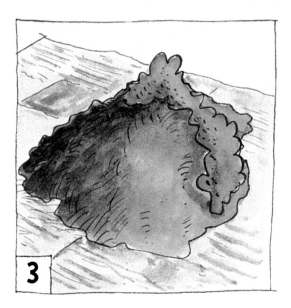

3

FACT FILE ▷▶

The acid vinegar reacts with the alkaline bicarbonate of soda to make a gas – carbon dioxide – which pushes the mixture up out of the bottle.

Using the funnel, pour the ketchup mixture into the buried bottle – and stand back!

Underwater Fountain

Create a colourful underwater show. Use any food colourings you like. If you haven't got a large bowl or tank you can use a jug and one bottle to make a solo show.

What you will need:

- large glass jug, a tank, or large clear plastic bowl
- 2-3 small glass bottles
- 2-3 different food colourings

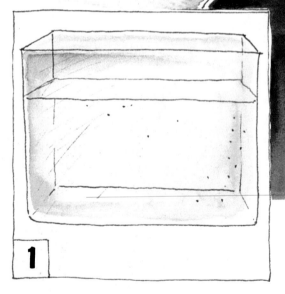

1

Pour cold water into the jug, bowl or tank until it is three-quarters full.

2

Fill the bottles with warm water and add a different colouring to each.

3

Place the bottles in the tank so that the tops are well below the surface. Now watch the swirling colourful show.

Upside-down Fountains

Drop ice cubes made from coloured water into a jug of cold water. At first they will float but, as the ice melts, coloured water will swirl downwards, as it is colder than the water around it.

Invisible Ink

Write up your scientific notes so that no one else can see them. You can use onion juice instead of lemon but you may cry a lot!

What you will need:

- 1 lemon
- small bowl or egg cup
- plain white paper
- fine paintbrush or old, empty fountain pen
- oven gloves or pair of kitchen tongs

007

1

Squeeze the lemon juice into the bowl or egg cup. Dip in your brush or pen and write on the paper.

2

3–5 mins

Ask a grown-up to help put the paper into an oven pre-heated to 170°C/325°F/Gas 3. Leave for 3-5 minutes.

3

Carefully remove the paper from the oven, using oven gloves or tongs. Take care — the paper is hot!

Keep any leftover lemon juice for writing more secret messages.

FACT FILE ▷▶
The heat of the oven 'burns' the lemon juice. This makes it reappear like magic.

Ectoplasmic Gunk

One minute this gunge behaves like liquid, then it's a solid — wacky stuff! Make as much of this as you like and use any food colouring you want.

What you will need:
- cornflour
- bowl
- jug of water with food colouring added
- tablespoon

Put some cornflour in the bowl and add a little coloured water. Stir well.

2 Gradually add more water until the gunk is about as thick as mayonnaise.

3 Jab in your spoon, or squish it in your hands, and it will feel solid. Stir it gently, or scoop some up in your hand, and it's liquid!

FACT FILE ▷▷

The ectoplasm behaves like a liquid when you treat it gently as all the particles of cornflour can slide around each other. Pushing it or squeezing it in your hands makes all the cornflour particles jam together and act like a solid.

Jumping Bugs

Static electricity turns these little insects into jitter bugs. You could try using bug or insect stickers on the paper instead of drawing your own.

What you will need:

- coloured tissue paper
- felt-tip pens or bug stickers
- scissors
- balloon

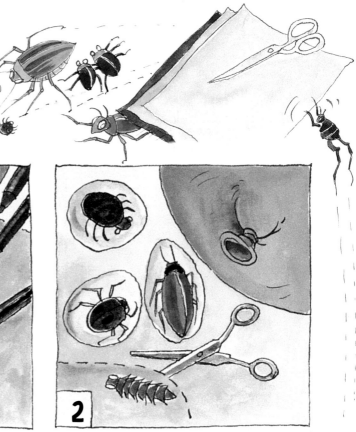

1 Draw some tiny bugs on the tissue paper or stick on your stickers. Make lots of them.

2 Cut them out and pile them up. Blow up the balloon and tie the end in a knot.

3

FACT FILE ▷▶

Static electricity is made when some materials are rubbed together – like a balloon against your hair or a woolly jumper. It is this kind of electricity that makes the paper jump towards the balloon.

Rub the balloon on top of your head or on your clothes. Hold it above the bugs and watch 'em jump.

Weird or What?

The average flea can jump 200 times its own height.
Just imagine how high we could jump if we were fleas!

Professor Brainstorm Cocktail

Impress your friends with this fantastic fizzer!
You probably have to be a mad scientist to drink it —
but it is quite safe to try a little.

What you will need:

- glass of cold water, three-quarters full
- few drops of food colouring (your choice of colour!)
- 1½ heaped tablespoons icing sugar
- 3 heaped teaspoons bicarbonate of soda
- 6 teaspoons lemon juice

Add the food colouring to the water. Give it a stir.

Do this where spills won't matter.

Stir in the sugar and bicarbonate of soda.

40

The acid lemon
juice and alkaline
bicarbonate react
to make a gas –
carbon dioxide
or CO_2. This is
the gas that puts
the fizz into
fizzy drinks.

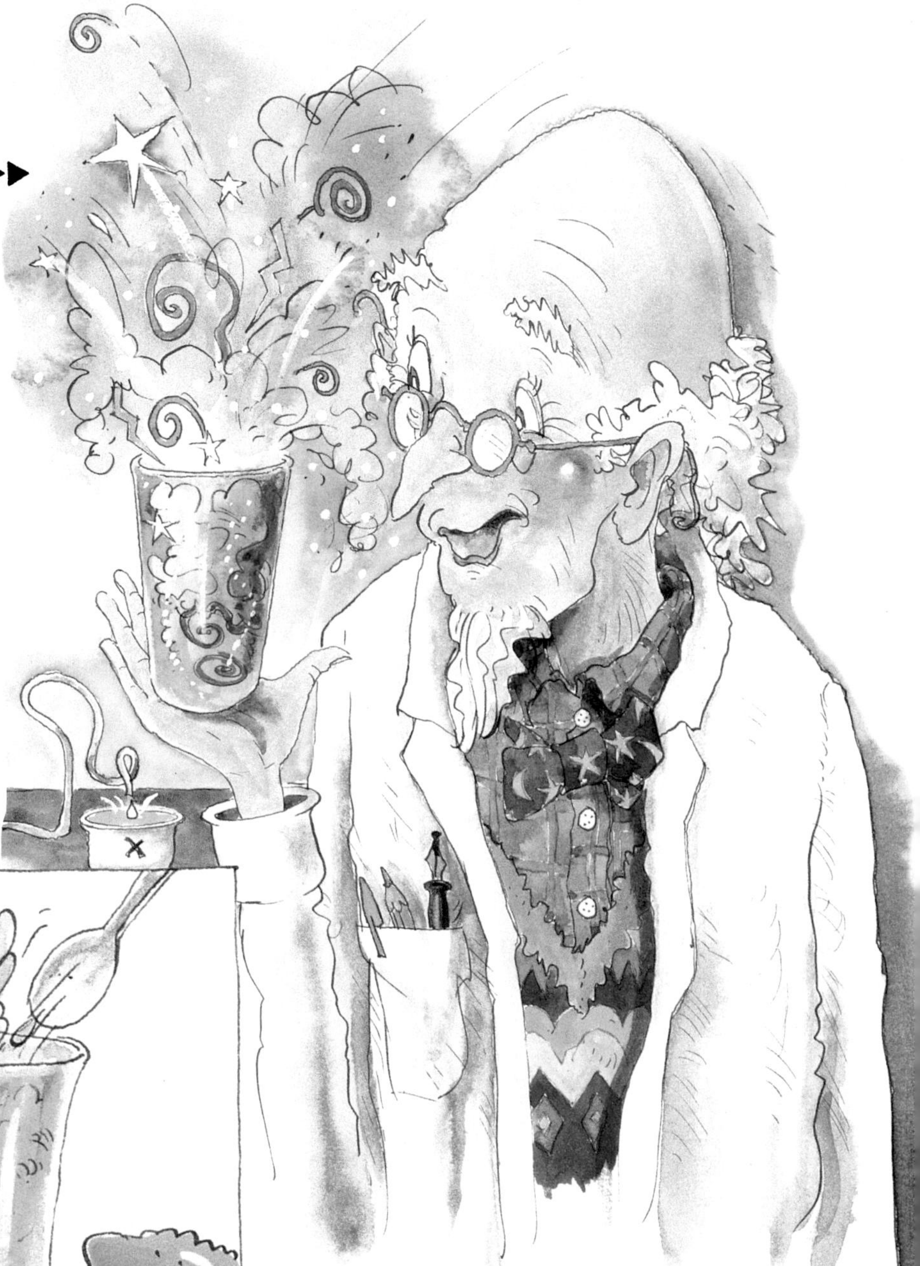

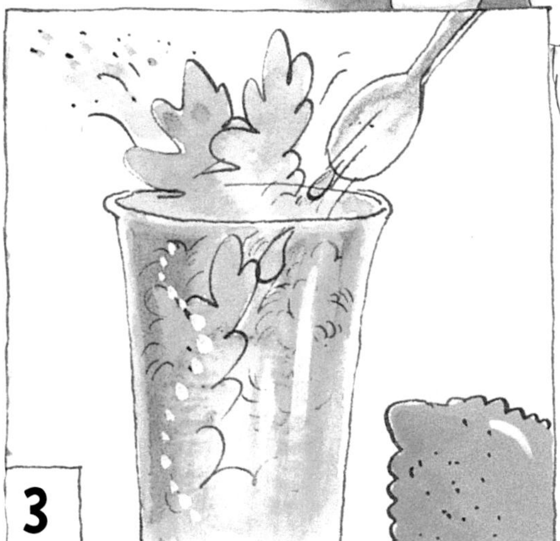

3

Finally add the lemon juice and
watch it whizz.

The Amazing Twister

This is very simple and very curly!

What you will need:

- sticky tape
- scissors
- heavy-duty kitchen foil
- small desk lamp

FACT FILE ▷▷

When metal is heated it expands, but plastic does not. When metal foil and plastic tape are stuck together, the expanding foil forces the tape into curls.

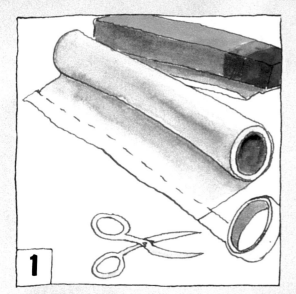

1

! Do not touch the light bulb with fingers or foil.

Carefully position a length of sticky tape along the edge of the foil. Trim it.

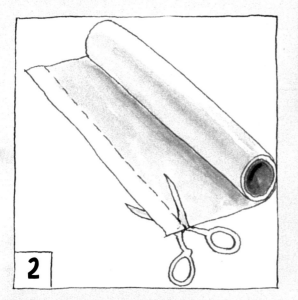

2

Cut off the strip of sticky tape with tinfoil stuck to one side.

3

Tape one end to a worktop or table and hold the lamp close to it. Just watch it start to curl and twist as the foil heats up.

Fake Fossil Footprint

Create a fascinating piece of fossil evidence. Make a cast of a footprint or weird shape to convince your friends that something strange and prehistoric once haunted the neighbourhood. You can use a muddy patch of garden instead of a box of sand.

What you will need:
- 1 cup of cold water
- 2 cups of plaster of Paris (from a builders' merchant)
- bowl or old plastic pot
- small cardboard box with about 7 cm of sand in it

Press the shape of your print into the sand or mud using your hands, feet or any other interesting-shaped object.

Pour the water into the bowl and sprinkle the plaster over it. Leave for 2 minutes. Then mix well with a clean hand to smooth any lumps. Leave for 4 minutes.

3

Pour the plaster into your shape, and clean the bowl straight away. Leave the plaster to set, then lift out your fossil evidence.

FACT FILE ▷▶

Fossils are the preserved remains or traces of plants and animals. Without them we would not know what prehistoric creatures looked like or when they lived. A trace fossil – like a dinosaur footprint – is the mark made by an animal while it was alive, preserved in later layers of soil and rock.

Pus-filled Boil

A gross experiment to test the nerve of your best friend.

What you will need:
- red and yellow (or green) food colourings
- some cottonbuds
- vaseline
- teaspoon
- small bowl or egg cup
- a tissue

Weird or What?

Your skin never stops growing. Dead skin falls off, takes the dirt with it, and more skin cells are constantly produced. About 4 kg of skin flakes off you every year. Dust is mostly made up of old bits of you!

Choose where you want your oozing boil to be, and paint or dab a little red food colouring on to the skin. Use a cottonbud.

Dead SKIN

FACT FILE ▷▶

Pus is putrid stuff. It is
made of infection-fighting
body fluids, dead cells,
and dead bacteria.

Use a fresh cottonbud
for mixing.

2

Mix a little vaseline with the
yellow or green colouring in the
bowl or egg cup. Put a blob on
the red food colouring patch.

3

Tear a single layer of tissue to fit
over the blob. Place on top and
seal the 'pus' inside, smoothing
down the edges of 'skin'.

Published by b small publishing ltd.
The Book Shed, 36 Leyborne Park, Kew,
Richmond, Surrey, TW9 3HA, UK
© b small publishing, 2000
This new edition published in 2012
1 2 3 4 5

Colour reproduction: Vimnice Printing Press Co. Ltd., Hong Kong
Printed in China by WKT Co. Ltd.
Editorial: Susan Martineau and Olivia Norton
Design: Lone Morton and Louise Millar
Production: Madeleine Ehm
With thanks to Phil White, Head of Science, Grey Court School, Ham.
ISBN 978-1-908164-62-9
British Library Cataloguing-in-Publication Data.
A catalogue record for this book is available from the British Library.

b small publishing

If you have enjoyed this book, look out for our other fun activity
books for young children.

Order them from any good bookshop or send for a catalogue to:
b small publishing ltd.
The Book Shed, 36 Leyborne Park,
Kew, Richmond, Surrey, TW9 3HA, UK
www.bsmall.co.uk
www.facebook.co.uk/bsmallpublishing @bsmallbear